Contents

COMMODIFYING HONOR IN FEMALE SEXUALITY – HONOR KILLINGS, ROLE OF JUDICIARY AND THE NEED FOR A SEPARATE DOMESTIC LEGISLATION

VOLUME 1, ISSUE 4 OF BRILLOPEDIA

S. MANJU PRIYA

ISBN 979-888530552-5

Preface

"Start writing, no matter what. The water does not flow until the faucet is turned on".

-Louis L'Amour

Hundreds of students and professors are contributing their work to Brillopedia, we are here to provide ample information about Law and Contemporary issues. Our aim is to provide a platform for today's generation to express their views and ideas on law and contemporary law.

Publication

This research paper is published in volume 1, issue 4 of Brillopedia

CHAPTER ONE

ABSTRACT

"Caste is a notion; it is a state of mind. The destruction of caste does not, therefore, mean the destruction of a physical barrier. It means a notional change"- Dr.B.R.Ambedkar.

Violence against women's autonomy, in all matters and especially in matters of sexuality and marriage, is one of India's most widespread and tenacious forms of gender violence and also the least recognized. It is a form of violence that hides in plain sight. Violence against both men and women to prevent a them from exercising their choice in love and marriage is not properly documented, since India does not have a specific law against "honor" crimes. To spot such violence and confront it, you need to look beneath the surface and read between the lines of available documentation. This is not possible when statistics of honor crimes are difficult to track with no specific definition of honor crime in place. There has been much debate about passing a legislation to specifically address honor crime through 242nd Law commission report. Through this paper the author analyses the existing legal framework to deal with such crime as well as how the judiciary has viewed this subject over the years. In this regard the author suggests for a separate legislation to combat honor crimes.

CHAPTER TWO

INTRODUCTION

Honor crimes are acts of violence, which may or may not result in murder are generally committed by the male members of the family against women in the family contending that they have brought dishonor upon their family and community at large. The use of word honor for such a dishonorable act is in itself ironic in nature as there is nothing honorable in such killings. In fact they are nothing but barbaric and shameful acts of murder committed by brutal, feudal minded persons. In the light of Supreme Court Judgment in **Shakti Vahini v Union of India**[1] it can be said the that honor based crimes can be due to various factors such as (i) loss of virginity outside marriage; (ii) pre-marital pregnancy; (iii) infidelity; (iv) having unapproved relationships; (v) refusing an arranged marriage; (vi) asking for divorce; (vii) demanding custody of children after divorce; (viii) leaving the family or marital home without permission; (ix) causing scandal or gossip in the community, and (x) falling victim to rape. One of the most viscous and widespread forms of gender violence that hides in plain sight is this violence against women's autonomy in matters of sexuality and marriage. However this violence despite being prominent against both men and women is not properly documented as there is no specific law against honor crimes. Thus this head led to one to look beneath the surface and read between lines of available documentation to spot such violence and thereby confront it. This is not possible when statistics of honor crimes are difficult to track with no specific definition of honor crime as well as due to statistics kept according to the type of crime as opposed to motive for the crime[2]. The debate is prevalent to pass a honour crime specific legislation (as the already existing laws to deal with this issue through criminal code[3], domestic violence Act[4] and Caste Atrocities Act[5] has made no significant impact) through 242nd Law commission report which suggested a legal framework for Prevention of Interference with Freedom of Matrimonial Alliance draft bill and Private member bill of 2017 introduced in Lok Sabha.[6] However nothing concrete has happened so far. However the judiciary has then and there come up with its intervention on a case to case basis. Further the under reporting of honor crimes as well as such crimes disguised as suicides or natural deaths all hint at one solution that is to have a formal legal framework to address this issue. Hence through this article the author analyses the feasibility of exclusive legislation to deal with such crimes. The author in this paper critically analyze the current legal framework and the role that judiciary has played to deal with such crimes to evaluate the need for a separate legislation in this regard."

[1] Shakti Vahini v. Union of India, (2018) 7 SCC 192

[2]United Nations High Commissioner for Refugees, *Refworld | India: Honour crimes, including their prevalence in both rural and urban areas; government protection and services offered to victims of honour crimes (2009-April 2013)*, Refworld , https://www.refworld.org/docid/ 51ab3f114.html (last visited Oct 24, 2020).

[3] Indian Penal Code,1860, § 299, § 300, § 301, No.45, Acts of Parliament,1860 (India)

[4] The Protection of Women from Domestic Violence Act, 2005, No.44, Acts of Parliament,2005(India)

[5] Scheduled Castes and Scheduled Tribes (Prevention of Atrocities) Act, 1989, No.33, Acts of Parliament,1989(India)

[6] The prevention of crimes in the name of honour and tradition and prohibition of interference with the freedom of matrimonial alliances bill, 2017

CHAPTER THREE

LEGAL ASPECTS AND EXISTING FRAMEWORK

The legal aspect of rights of an individual against honor killing can be seen in constitutional aspirations of equality right[1], right of prohibition of discrimination on religion and caste grounds[2], right to live and have personal liberty[3]. Even State policy's directive principles though not enforceable provides rights against honor killing that can be read through obligations of state to ensure proper livelihood of citizens[4] and to ensure youth to have a life free from material abandonment and exploitation[5]. Such crimes are alsoviolative of national legislations like1857's Indian Majority Act[6],Special Marriage Act,1954[7],Protection of Human Rights(Amendment)Act,2006 and Domestic violence Act,2005[8].

Though there is no specific legislations to deal with this crimes, its usually dealt under general provisions that is specified for homicide and manslaughter. Thus the existing framework includes provisions under the Indian Penal Code, that is,

- "Section 299-304 which deals with penalization of individuals either in guilt of murder or its culpability alone;
- Section 307 and 308 where the former penalizes attempt to murder in the process of committing such crimes and the later penalizes attempt to culpable homicide;
- Section 120A and B aiming to punish partied to conspiracies that's criminal in nature;
- Section 107-116 punishing persons for abetment of such offences;
- Section 34 and 35 penalizes acts done by several persons that criminal in nature and in the course to further a common intention of the parties.

[1] INDIA CONST. art.14

[2] INDIA CONST. art.15(1) & (3)

[3] INDIA CONST.art.21

[4] INDIA CONST. art.39(a)

[5] INDIA CONST.art.39(e) & (f)

[6] Indian Majority Act,1857,§ 3,No. 3, Acts of Parliament, 1857(India)- This section talks about the right to marry without any obstruction on the basis of caste, community or religion on attainment of majority, that is, 18 years.

[7] Practices of Honor killing runs contrary to the objective of the act which seeks to provide marriage irrespective of caste or religion.

[8] Domestic Violence Act, 2005, No.43, Acts of Parliament,2005(India)- The act considers it emotional abuse of women who's been prevented from choosing and marrying a life partner of their choice.

CHAPTER FOUR

INADEQUACIES OF THE CURRENT FRAMEWORK IN COMBATING HONOR CRIMES

One of the main limitations of the current framework is that its seriously handicapped on instances of honor crime leading to murder executed by mob or khappanchayats in which circumstances it becomes difficult to narrow down the culprit before the courts of law. Thus khappanchayat though playing an adverse role in acting as a legal system of its own mandating orders including that of execution against their own family which has major human rights implications are left scot free by the law agencies. KhapPanchayat are primarily a group of 5 prudent and powerful elderly chosen by the community, generally people of higher caste who are treated as kings and are classified generally on territorial jurisdiction basis There has been various instances where the Khappanchayat has basically operated as mere killer machines with no repercussions in upholding the honour of their community by regulating the conduct of people backing age old customs and practices[1]. Few of the barbaric acts of KhapPanchayats can be illustrated with instances such as "(i) Recorded events of checking the guilt of a women by mandating her to cook 'puris' in burning oil with bare hand and that if its done without burning her hands would be declared innocent; (ii) few other documented instances include cutting of ears or nose or hair of the accused accompanied by polishing of his/her face black and asked to run around naked in bare foot over a donkey's back; (iii) Instances of declaring women who are widows as demons and segregate them from community; (iv) Forcing coupled who marry outside their gothra to remarry against their wished as well ordering excommunication of the family members of the accused taking away their lands thereby pushing them in intolerable mental agony and humiliation."[2] What gives them this right even to the extend of murdering people in the name of honor? We can see how caste politics plays a major role in allowing such illegal bodies to function with zero intervention from government for violating law and order of country. Though the judiciary has tried on various occasions to uproot this institution, it still prevails to exist as KhapPanchyats retaining such redundant measures instilling and upholding the caste system is favorable vote bank politics that the politicians don't want to abolish. Further the ground reality is that these institutions are in terms with the police authorities where even the law agencies share the same prejudiced mindset of concepts of Dishonor and this makes it difficult for individuals to even get a case registered.

This failure in identification has made justice hard to get with none to very few neglibleamount of cases of FIR's filed by the police in this regard. Even if such cases are pursued, the conviction rate owing to stereotyping of judicial proceedings has made it hard to ever get justice the individual deserves. Another difficulty that strikes as a barrier in addressing the issues of honor crime is the stoic attitude of the both government and the courts to view honor killing as a separate offence to deal with its specific nature of the offence. This is because categorizing of offences on its nature of crime rather than the motivation of crime makes it hard for the law enforcement agencies to identify such crimes in the first place. Also until the late 2013, there was no record taken by the National Crime Records to have a separate record of crimes of honor killing to address it and thus the large extend of this crime if undervalued. Further the special marriage act of 1956 which is said to have implemented with the aim to facilitate marriages irrespective of caste thereby promote and validate inter-caste marriage has also has a serious limitation in reaching grassroots of rural areas where still informal courts such as panchayats play a major role in decision making on matters of community. Further the 30 day mandatory period window to provide for notice for solemnization of marriage under the act puts inter-caste couple who marries against their parents' wishes in a horrendous and vulnerable position.

[1]Divya Narayanan, *SC clips khappanchayat's wings on marriages. But how did they get these wings?,* THE PRINT (March 28th, 4:34 PM),

https://theprint.in/theprint-essential/sc-clips-khap-panchayats-wings-on-marriages/45326/

[2]Kavita Kachhwaha, *Khap Adjudication in India: Honouring the Culture with Crimes*, 6 12 (2011).

CHAPTER FIVE

GENDER STEREOTYPING, ROLE OF JUDICIARY AND ITS LIMITATIONS

With no specific law in place, the judiciary has indeed played a major role of intervention on case to case basis for such crimes can be seen from the 2006 case where the court held that Honor crimes are nothing but cold-blooded murder in order to combat that inter-caste marriages should be encouraged so that the social fabric of the country is strengthened. The illegal functioning of KhapPanchayat was also heavily criticized in the case of Laxmikachhwaha[1] a pubic interest litigation which drew attention of the country as well the courts to the illegal regimes of KhapPanchayat where the court called them as caste panchayat functioning in the name of honor to prey on the weaker sections of the society. While holding their jurisdiction to rule such acts as illegal in nature, the Rajasthan High Court also directed the state to prevent such abuse of social influence by mandating them to arrest, restrain and punish such illegal functioning of bodies. Some of other noteworthy decisions of the court can be seen in the case of State of UP v Krishna Master[2] where the court ruled sentence to life of those accused to have murdered family members in the name of honor; Sujit Kumar v State of UP[3] and Madhu Priya Singh v State of UP[4] where the court pointed out the inadequacies and failure of police authorities to take any action in this barbaric acts of these panchayats and thereby fail in their duty of upholding the law and 2011 apex court case[5] where the court sought to interpret laws on the matter of public concern in which the court held that family member of the couple who wishes to marry should be left alone and there is no right for the family and community members to instigated violence or harasses the couple; thereby held that Khappanchyats resorting to such acts in an institutionalized set up is illegal. Also in the landmark case of Shakti Vahini[6] the court has issued guidelines with preventive, remedial and punitive measures to tackle honor killing and also played an activist role in asking states to report as to what steps are taken by them in this regard to curb such violence

However while the judiciary has played such an active role, it can be ignored how even the law enforcement agencies from grassroots police to even judges are victims of gender stereotyping where when such belief when applied to the case affect negatively to recognize the enjoyment of rights of individual of the particular case. While such inferences due to personal bias are indeed prejudicial in nature, these when applied in cases of 'honor' decply affect the sexual and reproductive rights of women in maintaining their bodily autonomy. For example, some popular gender notions such as women are chaste and destined to be mothers can be directly linked to how the judges infer about an individual and thus affect the judgment's ability in effecting meaningful remedies. Such stereotyping also affects the voices, arguments and testimonies of women as parties as well witnesses as it affects and places doubts their credibility which can even lead judges to misinterpret and misapply laws[7]. Few results of such stereotyping can be seen through cases of **Tukaram v State of Maharasthra** where the a rape victim was subject to further stereotyping by the judge who allowed the past sexual history of the women to be read together with strict rules of corroboration and consent. Further in case of **Kamalanathha v state of Tamil Nadu[8]**, it can be observed how in addition to prosecution's burden of proof, the rape victim has the additional burden of 'performance' in accordance with the rigid image set by the judiciary of a 'Stereotypical Rape Victim' while in reality there is no typical common patterns of such victims. From the above instances it can be seen how prejudicial and preconceived beliefs of judges has played a major role in issuing such decisions where relevant facts are not taken into consideration and thus has resulted in adoption of rigid standards especially for women of the country in matters concerning their sexual autonomy and thus penalizing those who don't conform to such stereotyped beliefs of the individual.

[1]S.B. Criminal Misc. Petition No.1423/2013

[2]State Of U.P vs Krishna Master & Ors on 3 August, 2010, , https://indiankanoon.org/doc/572710/ (last visited Nov 27, 2021).

[3]Sujit Kumar And Ors. vs State Of U.P. And Ors. on 6 May, 2002, , https://indiankanoon.org/doc/1406726/ (last visited Nov 27, 2021).

[4]II (2004) DMC 294

[5]ArumugamServai v State of Tamil Nadu, (2011) 6 SCC 405

[6] Shakti Vahini v. Union of India, (2018) 7 SCC 192

[7]OHCHR | General Recommendations, , https://www.ohchr.org/EN/HRBodies/CEDAW/Pages/Recommendations.aspx (last visited Nov 25, 2021).

[8] (2005) 5 SCC 194

SUGGESTIONS AND THE NEED FOR SEPARATE LAW: IN THE LIGHT OF AIDWA's 2011 BILL and 2012 & 2015 LAW COMMISSION BILL

The first of its kind bill to deal with honor crimes was brought up by the All India Democratic Women's Association (AIDWA) in 2010 titled "The Prevention of Crimes in the Name of Honour and Tradition Bill" which seeked to address human rights violation of couples marrying outside of their caste and also seeked to enforce accountability on the part of police and administration. While this was pushed to the government, it got no reference to be tabled in the parliament. The law commission of India, through its 242nd report came up with its own bill with a conservative approach to such crimes titled "Prohibition of Unlawful Assembly (Interference with the Freedom of Matrimonial Alliances) Bill, 2011." This bill aimed to control and put an end to unlawful assemblies mainly by khappanchayats with the intention to intimidate consenting adults to marry. While the law commissions consultation paper rejected the proposal of government to amend section 300 of IPC reasoning that difference of motivation of offences cant justify for a new provision and that the already existing provision are adequate to deal with crimes of murder; it however said there's a need to prevent such unlawful assemblies. There has also been the recent 2015 "The prohibition of Interference with the Freedom of Matrimonial alliances in the name of Honour and Tradition Bill" with intent to protect interests of personal liberty, right against victimization and also seeks to prohibit unlawful assemblies. However it is to be noted that none of these have resulted in a national legislation. However taking cue from these bills and international commitments that our country has made, the author provides following suggestions:

- There is a need to make honor killing a separate category of offence under Section 300 of IPC which includes a new definition for crimes resulting in murder, so that the already undocumented crimes of such nature would be addressed better by the law enforcement bodies with better clarity. There should also be separate punishment prescribed for such offence. However such an intervention through separate category should address not just inter-caste or inter-religion marriages that result in such crimes but also any kinds of marriage between the same castes also since there is tussle between the sub-caste within the same caste itself.

- There can be protection powers given to District level magistrates with a mandatory special cell of Police to protect the couples fleeing such intimidation from families. The law should also provide for accountability of these parties on default or omission of their duties under the act. Further when such crimes are committed, the investigation by police should primarily involve a caste angle first.

- There should be social initiatives and sensitization done mandatorily first for all law enforcement agencies to see beyond existing stereotyping of gender and social norms; secondly to rural areas and society at large to curb this acts and nib it at bud through social means. To combat honor crimes there is an urgent need for all stakeholders to come together in addressing the issue which should also be the goal of the new law.

- Further, the vulnerability of couples in waiting for almost 45 days to get their marriage registered under the Special marriage Act should be addressed so that this time is relaxed for such instances where period time for registration can be reduced to one week

- There should also be separate fast track courts be constituted in this regard to speed up the proceedings

- The law should be widened to not only include the individual executing the murder but also the person giving such orders. This is because this crime needs a different kind of approach than the usual way under section 300 of IPC which doesn't take into consideration the motive behind the murder. When such is the case, in crimes of these starting from Khaps to own families of the victims are themselves planners and perpetrators in such crimes. Thus joint liability for all these parties should be made compulsory to effectively tackle such crimes. Also on the same lines, the Indian Evidence Act should be amended to transfer the burden of proof to the accused including khaps to prove their innocence.

- Further the law shouldn't end with just punishment of wrong doers but also ensure adequate compensation, rehabilitation packages as well as economic schemes to uplift them and help them rebuild their lives.

- Due to the structural inequalities and power nexus that prevails in the society, the state must also ensure special protection to witnesses and whistle blowers till the end of court proceedings.

- Further the states should honor their obligations made under various human rights treaties such as CEDAW to eliminate gender stereotyping including that of judiciary that stands in the way in achieving justice. This is because such stereotyping also goes against the fair trial ensuring equality before the court which is a right of every individual under the International Covenant on Civil and Political Rights[1](ICCPR). Thus by honoring this the state should take steps in sensitization of judges to ensure (i) they don't engage in stereotyping (obligation to respect); (ii) they make sure such stereotyping don't result in infringement of human rights of victims (obligation to protect); (iii) to conform to rights of individuals to have a proceeding and judgment free from wrongful stereotyping of judges (obligation to fulfill)[2].

[1] Article 12,ICCPR,United Nations High Commissioner for Refugees, *Refworld | International Covenant on Civil and Political Rights*, Refworld , https://www.refworld.org/docid/3ae6b3aa0.html (last visited Nov 24, 2021).

[2]United Nations High Commissioner for Refugees, *Refworld | General Recommendation No. 28 on the Core Obligations of States Parties under Article 2 of the Convention on the Elimination of All Forms of Discrimination against Women*, Refworld , https://www.refworld.org/docid/4d467ea72.html (last visited Nov 24, 2021).

CHAPTER SEVEN

CONCLUSION

From the above it is concluded mere provisions of Indian Penal Code prohibiting such crimes won't effect a change in the society. There is an urgent need for a separate legislation addressing this crime in particular where all shareholders starting from police officials, judiciary, NGO's, family members and society as a whole should come together to combat such crime. A comprehensive legislation is a must to address the unique nature of the crime and to really target the perpetrators of such crime for prosecution. The KhapPanchayats's assumption that it has a role to moderate such practices against such couple needs to be specifically addressed through strict piece of legislation banning them from such unlawful assemblies perpetrating immoral acts. It is also observed that the state should take upon itself the duty to regularly sensitize the general public as well the judiciary to re-think their patriarchal values of the society and to abolish caste system and encourage inter-caste and inter-religious marriages to strengthen the social fabric of the society. Public at large should also be educated about the rights guaranteed to them under the constitution and how to claim them. While law in itself can only be used to punish the criminal, the real change to remove the crime depends on the mentality of people and thus change needs to begin from our homes.